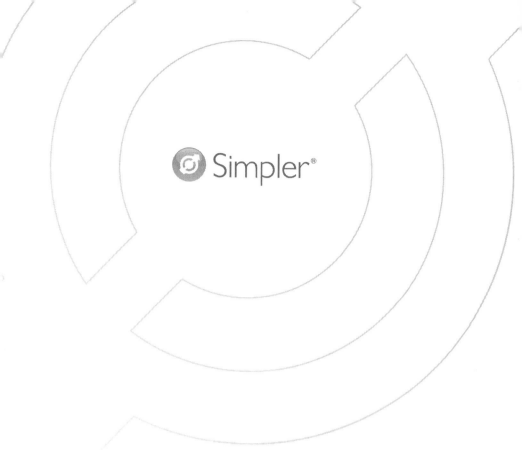

THE LITTLE
BOOK OF LEAN

THE BASICS

Chris Cooper

Table of Contents

ISBN:1475218354

ISBN-13: 9781475218350

The Little Book of Lean, Published 2011 by Simpler Consulting, L.P.

For more information contact:

Simpler Consulting
P.O. Box 1291
Bloomfield, IA 52537

www.simpler.com

© 2011 Simpler Consulting, L.P.

Dedication

My work has taken me all around the world by land, sea and air, and my clients have taught me many things, but I never doubt that the best day's work I ever did was finding my wife Nicki, without whom this book would not have moved beyond the "good idea" stage. With you and our children, Elliott and Louis, I am never lost for inspiration.

My Thanks

An author has nothing to write about without experiences and inspiration.

My thanks are therefore due to my inspirational mother and father who taught me that anything is possible, and there is no time like NOW to start. Growing up in such positive surroundings predisposed me to what has become my life's work.

Pat, Jack and Gavin South deserve similar praise for becoming my second family when, at 16 years of age, I thought I had outgrown my own. BAE Systems gave this 16-year-old kid an opportunity in the form of an apprenticeship while sponsoring my part-time education. As if this was not enough, they then gave me opportunity after opportunity as my industrial career unfolded.

It was Kawasaki Heavy Industries that inducted me into what I call the "Toyota School of Improvement." Their ever-improving products, along with Suzuki, Yamaha and Honda, gave me inspiration to research and study the Japanese Quality Movement more deeply. Bernard Taylor was an inspiration on a daily basis as he stretched my then theoretical knowledge into practical application. There is nothing like the thrill of transforming a business (for the better) to get you out of bed each morning. For that, Trevor and Pauline Bryan, thank you.

When I had tired of my aerospace career, Jim Womack and Sid Joynson provided the timely kick I needed to become a teacher and coach of this stuff in my own right, and Simpler Consulting was the place where the most exciting work assignments and best people could be found. George Koenigsaecker, Doug Goschke, Ed Constantine, and Nick Middleton gave me opportunity beyond measure. It was during my early days with Simpler I came across Steven Spear who I knew instantly was not your normal Toyota researcher. Like me, he understood from the start that there is a whole lot more to this stuff than a bunch of tools. It was after a phone conversation with Steve that I literally put pencil to paper.

Simpler's Glyn Finney & Katy Dowd deserve thanks for being the completer-finishers I struggle to be. Lastly, my thanks go out to the Ex-Danaher Executives to whom I have apprenticed myself. They have helped me learn how the Lean approach can be well-applied at an enterprise level even if you are not Japanese and you don't make cars.

Introduction

When I started my Lean journey over 20 years ago, I was soon aware there was so much to the approach that it would probably take me a lifetime to master it. Indeed, along the way each twist and turn has proven the need for constant personal learning, yet right from the start I was also struck by how simple the basic principles are. In the early days before the Toyota School of Improvement was called Lean Thinking, I had to go to a host of sources to "see the whole," but once having seen the elements in practice there was mentally no turning back.

History and hindsight have now taught us that in essence what we were doing all along was two things:

1.) Improving the world of work using the principles of the Toyota Production System,

while simultaneously

2.) Changing the enterprise culture to one akin to the Toyota Way

Successful transformations did both things while the unsuccessful typically applied only pieces of principles and, therefore, failed.

Having said that, given that the fundamentals are so simple and so much has been written about Lean, or what should perhaps more accurately be called the Toyota School of Improvement, it has been a constant source of frustration to me that the subject of Lean seems to have become only more complicated by further thought, abstraction and writing. I suspect this is because most of the thinking and writing that has been done regarding Lean has been without much in the way of actual doing.

So to assure you of what you are about to read, I can say that 100% of what I have written comes from actual hands-on experience of doing this stuff. My words are the product of lessons learned along the way in many varied organizations. From military to industry to non-profit, I have yet to find a place of work where Lean principles do not apply and whose people are not amazed at what can be achieved. Indeed, if there is a first lesson, then it is this: only when you take a theory and actually DO, does the real learning begin.

My motivation and aims for this book are very simple. Generally, Lean is not taught to enough current or future generations of leaders so I wanted to distill my knowledge to its basic essence so that many more can apply it.

What I really want is to set readers on a path of action that shows a way of looking at the world of human work. Once a person can "see", it is truly beautiful to behold – a platform to demonstrate the infinite potential we human beings have. This should be inspiration enough for every reader to begin to forever improve!

Chris Cooper 2011

Using This Book

For each key element of the book I have added a sensei question designed to stimulate your thinking. It is my hope that you will use the space to add value to your own personal copy of the book by making notes based on your own reflections. I look forward to discussing your thoughts, notes and actions with you in the future.

My Simple Starting Definitions

Doing Lean: "Continuous improvement of the flow of value via the elimination of waste by the people who do the work, in their workplace, under the caring guidance of a teacher"

Given that the majority of practitioners do not start from a "greenfield" site or have an already Toyota-like culture, then a definition of *Lean Transformation* is required:

"Changing the way an enterprise approaches improvement and views its potential such that collectively, people create ever-improving results and a culture in which Lean principles are routinely practiced and supported forever"

Finally, I have learned that Lean transformation must be led, so L*ean leadership* is:

"The creation of direction that results in an environment in which every member of the enterprise is nurtured and encouraged to practice Lean principle-based improvement in support of True North Goals"*

*True North Goals include four metrics: Human Development, Quality, Time and Financial.

Precepts

I have learned the hard way that Lean cannot take hold in any lasting sense without the acceptance of the following precepts:

1. Dissatisfaction with the Status Quo
2. Humility
3. Respect for people, society, and the environment
4. A belief that Lean works wherever work is done
5. "Gemba" wisdom that is valued over theoretical knowledge
6. Leadership that believes all of the above

These precepts should be memorized.

1. **Dissatisfaction with the status quo**

2. **Humility**

3. *Respect for individuals, society and the environment*

4. *A belief that Lean works wherever work is done*

5. *Gemba wisdom that is valued over theoretical knowledge*

6. *Leadership that believes all of the above*

Never use the absence of these conditions or precepts as an excuse for not starting because we act our way into a new set of beliefs over time. Indeed, the only barrier to starting is that these precepts have to be something the people in the enterprise **_want_** to learn. I call this the "pull" for Lean, and without such a pull implementing Lean is a very hard thing to do.

Sensei Question #1

What is the current condition in your organization with regard to the Precepts?

Sensei Question #2

What do you think you need to do about that?

Start Lean with a Clear Reason

Even though my first question is always "Why do you want to use Lean?" I never fail to be surprised when people seem to want to be Lean for Lean's sake. It's helpful to use the famous 5-whys technique to discover our reasons.

Question 1: Why did I personally get started with Lean?

Answer 1: It was simply to make things better than they already were.

Question 2: But why did I want to make things better than they were?

Answer 2: Because I could not see us achieving our business goals using the same methods and processes

Question 3: Why couldn't I achieve our goals using the same methods and processes?

Answer 3: Because our current improvements (at the time based on automation and computerization) were not producing enough net results to the bottom-line

Question 4: Why was that?

Answer 4: Because each individual improvement was focused only on a tiny part of the entire flow and seemed to only make things hit the next queue faster

Question 5: Why was that?

Answer 5: Because our prevailing improvement philosophy at that time was like our organization – departmentalized and, except for a handful of improvement specialists, no one was expected to make improvement except the bosses

Years ago our performance as an organization rarely met our goals and so when I was exposed to the principles of the Toyota School of Improvement I believed I had seen a better way that was more likely to succeed in the long term. I was sold on the ideas and principles. In these days of global competition it is rare to find an organization that does not have a compelling need for a Lean approach to achieve their goals, but leadership still has to make the reason clear, and at minimum, link their application of Lean to strategy and goals.

The best leaders will do that via a method called *Strategy Deployment*.

Know Waste before Claiming to Know Work

In order to do any Lean implementation it is imperative to understand and work with the twin concepts of value and waste.

"Waste is any activity that requires time or resources without creating value for the customer."

1. Activities that harm people
2. Over-producing; doing more than is required right now
3. Waiting – for anything to arrive
4. Movement – of stuff
5. Over processing
6. Inventory
7. Unnecessary motion for people
8. Defective work and its associated detection and re-work

Wastes are caused by evolution or design of process so they can be only be removed by evolution and design. Waste as the biggest opportunity for improvement is a simple concept and one which gets people fired up once they can see it. But before rushing off to become a waste warrior, answer these questions:

Sensei Question #3

Can you make a list of examples of the eight wastes found in your home?

Sensei Question #4

Now make a list of examples of these eight wastes at your workplace.

Sensei Question #5

To whom does the waste belong in each case?

Understand Value before You Can Eliminate Waste

Value-adding work is what remains once all wasteful activities have been eliminated. Every *value proposition* that we produce as a product or service is, in essence, a proposed solution to a problem.

Whether or not there is *value* in a solution can only be truly understood through the eyes of the customer.

We humans are only too ready to assume <u>we</u> understand value without actually asking customers and, unfortunately, most customers typically only know how to ask for slight variations of what they currently see. Consequently, really understanding value can only come from dialogue and truly exploring customer needs in their environment. As a sensei it is my role to help people "hear" the Voice of the Customer (VOC) and "read" the Environment of the Customer (EOC).

 In most cases that I come across the true essence of the value is starkly simple; it is only too often over-complicated by the presence of waste!

NOTE: Given that *value* and *waste* can be very personal and people are often defined by both the work they do and the value choices they make, be careful not to offend. It is easy to do so with the dangerous combination of low sensitivity and newly-born improver's zeal!

Sensei Question #6

What is the value provided by your organization?

Sensei Question #7

Can you distill the value down to the essence of a verb and noun?

Sensei Question #8

What problem does the value you produce resolve for customers?

Focus Improvement on Waste – Wherever Work is Done

Once a person can truly see work as elements of waste and value-added, there is always more waste than value-added work. So it follows logically that if improvements eliminate waste, then the results gained will be greater. In contrast, improving the value-added steps of work is usually costly and more difficult to do. Further, when considered end-to-end, improving the value-added steps alone typically yields little in terms of end-to-end results.

Eliminating waste gets big results and often with no more investment than a change of mindset and practice.

So why doesn't everyone do this? Because most people have been subconsciously brainwashed over time to see all activity as work and "just the way it is around here." Not so for Lean thinkers, who see that ALL WORK = VALUE-ADDED ACTIVITIES + WASTE.

Unfortunately in most workplaces the brainwashing starts from the moment any innocent enters the place of work and starts asking "why?" Each answer, if accepted, builds a layer of blindness and ultimately the current state of things is rationally explained even though, when considered as a whole, it makes no sense.

Sensei Question #9

Which approach to improvement is most practiced in your place of work?

Sensei Question #10

Ask yourself the Five Whys to the answer you gave in Question 9.

Sensei Question #11

Who owns and leads the method of improvement used?

Learn to See Waste

Techniques to see waste can be used in any workplace. Unfortunately, traditional process maps and documented procedures do not discern between value and waste. The good news is that with proper guidance they can be re-detailed to reveal waste. These **Value Stream Maps** can, and should, be done at every level of the organization on an annual basis.

Such maps should only be produced via direct observation in the actual workplace. Once the eyes have been trained to "see" they will notice many wasteful steps. A Value Stream Map is essential to put the observed waste into its overall context.

An **ideal state map** (where only the value-adding steps remain) should then be completed immediately after the current state to establish an idea of what's possible in the long term and remove the notion that a small change will suffice to make breakthrough improvement.

Finally, a **future state map** under the guidance of an experienced coach will set the next improvement challenge and help create the plan to achieve it. Doing this future state annually embeds the habit of *forever improve*. Annual use of Strategy Deployment helps provide the drive for results and the imperative to implement the future state.

Sensei Question #12

Value Stream Maps have to be conducted backwards. Can you think of five reasons why?

Sensei Question #13

What is it that should be flowing free from waste in your organization?

You must have a Routine Rhythm of Big Improvements Combined with the Daily Habit of Small Improvements

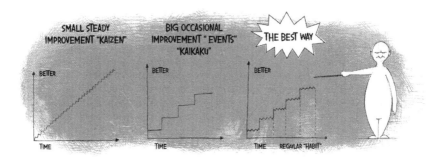

To realize a future state in anything but a greenfield site, we have to make system-wide change in a structured sequence of events. The outcomes of such events are never perfect so we also have to make small daily improvements to make progress. My experience is that without this blend of routine big change and small changes there is no chance of continuous progress. The rhythm has to become a habit, **and** ultimately, a belief of the enterprise; otherwise, the long term improvement potential promised in the ideal state will never be reached and, worse still, sustaining hard-earned improvements will be impossible.

Whether by events or "just-do-its," improvement should be done right away.

Try-storming not *Brainstorming* is the ideal. Too often we brainstorm our way into inaction!

I have also learned over the years there is really no such thing as *sustainment* . . . only improvement or decline.

Sensei Question #14

How would you describe your organization's improvement routine?

Sensei Question #15

What is the difference between Discipline and Habit?

What Happens when Waste is Eliminated?

Upon seeing value and waste, the whole world of human endeavour becomes a world of processes. Over time the student of Lean will be able to define, create and link processes, and also be able to discern and classify processes by types, understanding the general levels of waste they contain. As waste is eliminated, processes will evolve up the following hierarchy:

The Artisan type – Work is conducted by an individual to his/her own standards and methods. Output is only repeatable to the degree achievable by human memory. This style is only really appropriate in a one-person enterprise with no long term plan.

The Craft type – Work is conducted by a group of individuals to agreed standards and some common methods. Output is more repeatable than by Artisan approaches but highly dependent on each individual. Each individual typically requires and owns a full set of tools / equipment.

The Mass Production type – Work is arranged to flow and is subjected to the division of labor. Each task is performed to exacting standards and methods. Output pace is pushed on the basis of forecasted needs and the system is run according to beliefs rooted in the principles of *economies of scale* and *economic batch quantities*. When coupled with standard cost accounting, in many cases individual equipment or sub-process efficiency is unwittingly pursued often to the detriment of overall system efficiency. Output is much more repeatable than the Artisan or Craft types but requires a certain volume to be cost effective which, in many cases, seldom matches actual demand or its variation. Inventory Management, Warehousing, Logistics, and Marketing promotions are all Non-Value Adding methods used as buffers to cope with this.

Respect for people is characteristically low in the mass production process. As "cogs in the machine," people are rarely encouraged to think beyond the narrow confines of their own jobs. In addition, most improvements or responses to problems are the responsibility of managers or people higher in the organization than those who do the value-added work. Improvement in this type of process is nearly always capital intensive and requires a high degree of system-level thinking to ensure that improvement in one area does not create waste in another. The human downside of the industrial revolution of mass production was so notorious that many sectors never embraced the model. Yet despite its shortcomings, millions of people have enjoyed decades of consistently high quality outputs and ever-reducing costs.

The Just-In-Time Flow Process

The Just-In-Time (JIT) division of labor, especially to the untrained eye, looks a lot like the mass production type of process; however labor is organized flexibly to match required output at a variety of tempo scenarios set by actual demand, not forecast. Inventory is deliberately held low and then progressively lowered to reveal problems, and thusly, opportunities to improve. Human skills are typically much higher. As the enterprise's collective ability to solve problems improves, then inventory can theoretically be lowered to the ideal of only what is needed at a given moment in time.

The labor force, as well as being placed to enable flow, is highly flexible and widely trained for an ability to adjust to different demand scenarios. A collection of **standard work scenarios** is used by workers to respond to demand. Activity is only triggered on-demand and quality is highly repeatable. Equipment is right-sized and flexible, and economies of scale-thinking gives way to "economies of Flow."

In contrast to the mass production process, the Just-in-Time flow-based process elevates respect for people engaged at all levels of the work. The flexibility of JIT demands broader skills, and having lower work-in-progress inventory means the whole end-to-end process is more visible and thus, understood by all. Greater skills and understanding give workers greater ownership of the process, more voice and higher work satisfaction. When job flexibility is combined with wide-scale involvement in the elimination of waste, the human spirit of the workforce is fully engaged.

Additionally, end-to-end understanding can be used as a basis for the improvement of the whole system by a much larger pool of knowledgeable people. This increase in the amount of effort and thinking that can be brought to bear on improvement means that more people have improvement of the process as part of their working lives. Because of this higher level of engagement, the rate of problem solving and improvement increases dramatically over the mass production type processes.

Sensei Question #16

Consider different sectors in your nation's economy; what is the dominant process style, and why?

Go with the Flow

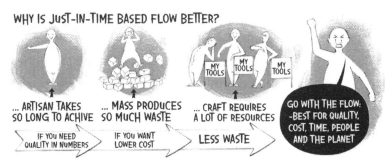

WHY IS JuST-IN-TIME BASED FLOW BETTER?

... ARTISAN TAKES SO LONG TO ACHIEVE — IF YOU NEED QUALITY IN NUMBERS — ... MASS PRODUCES SO MUCH WASTE — IF YOU WANT LOWER COST — ... CRAFT REQUIRES A LOT OF RESOURCES — LESS WASTE — GO WITH THE FLOW: -BEST FOR QUALITY, COST, TIME, PEOPLE AND THE PLANET

Even after centuries of evolution from Artisan to JIT Flow processes, many sectors still operate to essentially Craft process principles. We can theorize about why that is and argue about the strength of competitive pressures in certain sectors, but I prefer to assume things are the way they are because, a) They were good enough for the organization to succeed; and, b) Customers have not demanded or understood that there may be a different way.

This has led to some strange market paradoxes. For example, many of today's consumers unconsciously associate "craft made" with higher quality, despite most consumers having a lifetime of enjoying mass produced consistency. Highly regarded luxury brand producers have long since abandoned the personalized handcrafted products or services that made their names and have had to deal with new customers who are highly intolerant of the character that used be a by-product of a craft approach.

The rarity of craft/artisan production is still prized but production quality in use or experience is now presumed as a given. For a small number of pioneers (most notably post-war Toyota), the dream of high quality at low volume, without high cost yet available on demand, configured specific to customer order has become possible. Post-mass production consumers want the high quality that they have become accustomed to, configured to their personal needs and, except for the very affluent, at a price similar to the mass-produced offering. What is still surprising to me is how little the wider world of work has been affected by this process type shift. Why?

I have learned that without a compelling reason to do otherwise, most work processes will remain in their current state pretty much forever unless either a competitor emerges or a forward thinking leader drives the organization forward to a higher performance level.

Sensei Question #17

What would Just-In-Time flow look like in a hospital?

My Simple Starting Definitions

Just-In-Time Flow is the process type we inevitably arrive at when we continually subject our processes to the elimination of waste. In post-war Toyota this was not an accident. They needed to match the productivity of the Ford Mass Production System but serve the then-tiny volumes and individual needs of the Japanese market. Kiichiro Toyoda, in fact, first proposed his Just-in-Time concept in 1938 after visiting Ford and seeing the inherent wastes in Ford's Mass Production System.

However, it took more than three decades of progressive waste elimination for Toyota, led by Taiichi Ohno, to fully realize the JIT concept in Toyota manufacturing operations. Though the system contributed to Toyota's unrelenting rise in the industry, the general public remains largely unaware of the role JIT thinking has played; and indeed, to the untrained eye a Toyota plant looks pretty much like a Ford plant. The Toyota system that now makes such enormous volumes of vehicles it is actually, at its most fundamental roots, designed for making small volumes in high variety. Visual differences between Toyota's JIT and classic mass production systems are mostly unnoticeable, however looking at Toyota's financial performance since World War II yields a dramatic contrast in cost and profitability.

How to Adopt Just-In-Time

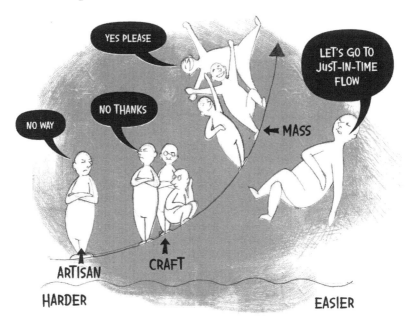

Unless talking about a greenfield site, the adoption of JIT is a major culture change which may well take three decades to become fully embraced. Processes are easy to change; habits and beliefs take much longer. This is because as waste is eliminated people have to un-learn the norms of the prevailing process type and adopt JIT process norms. In many cases workers may have deep resistance to what they perceive the future process to be.

For example, in a Mass-type process it will seem a small, but generally positive journey to move to JIT processes, but for a person in an Artisan or Craft-based process it will not. Why?

Most people who work in Craft-based processes unconsciously see personal value and skill in being able to negotiate the waste that is a fundamental part of their work. In many cases they are rated and rewarded for this ability. Not only have they grown accustomed to waste being there, but it often defines them as a worker. People who work in Craft-type process environments rarely work in a true team in the JIT-flow sense of the word, and what they think of flow is mostly influenced by the well-documented downsides of Mass Production. This is, therefore, a major part of the transformation task – securing enough hearts and minds to give things a try, work through the inevitable issues, and teach in a way that minimizes the trauma of such profound change.

Sensei Question #18

From which process type will your organization start as you begin your journey?

Sensei Question #19

What will it take to secure a commitment to move to flow-based processes?

The Foundational Elements of Just-In-Time Flow

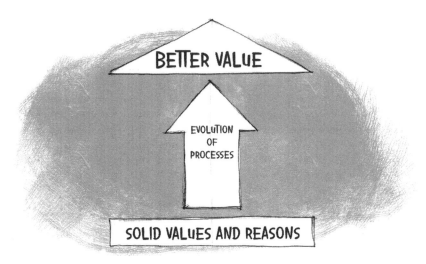

If we are to repay the trust that people give us to try something new, then it helps if we know what we are doing.

To evolve processes to Just-in-Time Flow is usually harder than everyone thinks it should be. Even a closer look at processes fails to discover some fundamental elements that have to be implemented in sequence and with each other.

If any of the following elements is missing, our transformation will hit trouble. I have written these elements deliberately in this sequence; as to do so matches what we typically find is the best and most effective way to impact long term culture and to get pay-as-you-go results. Sure, some people implement these elements in different sequence, but I and others have learned **by doing** why the following sequence is best.

1. Six S
2. One-item-flow
3. Right-sized equipment / changeover reduction
4. Takt – time driven standard work
5. Work is pulled, not pushed through the system
6. Visual management and Jidoka thinking
7. Team and Gemba-based problem solving
8. Cost management with job security
9. Total Productive Maintenance (TPM)
10. Leveling

Here is a breakdown of the elements and how they impact JIT flow:

1) Six S

This is a frighteningly simple concept that has wide-ranging benefits. It is usually seen by the novice as simple housekeeping, but to the trained eye is a highly visual barometer of overall progress. It was used as a test by early Japanese teachers to determine if learners "had what it took" to adopt the whole philosophy. I trust by the end of this chapter, the value of these practices will be clear.

The Six S's are a translation of six Japanese words and one Western word which, when used as principles to organize the workplace, make it easier to see and eliminate waste. At the same time, if implemented correctly 6S saves money and also builds a culture capable of the rest of the transformation.

1.1 Sort – Separate out things that are needed to operate the process from things that are not.

Human beings have a tendency to collect and hoard things over time, "just in case." Sort sets the basic discipline of using only what is needed, when it is needed. This is a subtle but foundational belief for the whole Lean concept.

1.2 Set in Order for Flow – Arrange equipment and human resources for the value to flow through the process with minimal waste.

When looking at processes from the point of good flow, waste between value added steps begins to look wrong-headed.

1.3 Shine – Clean everything to the point where the team can visually and immediately detect abnormal from normal conditions.

1.4 Standardize – Assign responsibility and agreed visual standards for keeping 6S going.

Note: The standards must be set by those committing to keep them.

1.5 Safety – Ensure every part of the process is safe

1.6 Sustainment – Learn the habits and discipline required to keep it up forever.

Once 6S is in place the team <u>should</u> be struggling with sustainment of JIT, especially with the new flow-based process as this provides a natural pull for the next elements. Too often I have seen 6S implemented with 1.2 being taught as "straighten" or "set in order." This is faking 6S and provides no impetus to do the rest of the elements; hence, I need to stress SET IN ORDER FOR FLOW.

Sensei Question #20

After implementing 6S the flow keeps stopping?
Why do you think this is?

2) One-Item-Flow

Consider the difference between Subway™ and McDonalds™. Subway flows their product through their process, step-by-step, allowing customers to configure at each step, their food on demand. It enables Subway to create a relatively tailored product while operating with almost zero inventory. McDonalds, by comparison, makes a standard product produced to satisfy a forecasted demand in batches.

At busy times the people in Subway work as a labor-divided team, each doing a part of the process; at less busy times with fewer customers to serve and fewer workers required, each does more of the process. If we go there when demand is very low, we may have the same person do the whole job from start to finish. In McDonalds, people have specific tasks and specialties; they work at their stations just as in mass production.

If my processes are currently mass production-influenced like McDonalds, then changing to one-item-flow will appear or feel less efficient at first. If I am used to craft-based processes it may take quite a while to think through how to organize and adapt the workplace and methodology to adopt flow.

Note: Most office-based processes are entirely craft-based. The guidance of a teacher in the workplace is essential here because often people can only think of reasons why "it won't work."

Sensei Question #21

**One-item-flow will stop whenever there is a problem.
Why is this a good thing?**

Sensei Says:

"The more we stop the better we get!" What are your thoughts on this?

3) Right-Sized Equipment / Changeover Reduction

One of the barriers to flow is caused by the current equipment that is in use. What is the value created by the equipment we use to do our work?

In an office environment, which is better for flow, the large complicated photocopier that always seems to be jammed and/or out-of-toner or the smaller device we have at home next to our PC? Our views of equipment efficiency are informed by economies of scale-thinking.

Right-sized equipment thinking, on the other hand, seeks to run only at the pace of demand. It seeks single-function equipment for maximum flexibility and small scale to fit right in the flow. Optimally, it is easy to maintain or move, and hence, it is usually smaller and lower cost than the "monuments" found in mass-type processes.

A Craft environment usually has more than enough right-sized equipment already. Those who work in a Mass process environment will likely have to wait until the next capital cycle to change to right-sized equipment. So, until then they will have to eliminate as much waste as possible from the set-up and changeover times so their "monuments" are not driven to large batches of work. This will reduce the belief in economic batch quantity-thinking and free the collective mind up for flow.

Sensei Question #22

What right-sized equipment has Subway developed in order to have equipment placed right in the flow?

Sensei Question #23

What pieces of your equipment will you need to right-size?

4) TAKT Time-Driven Standard Work

Without a standard way of doing things there is no basis upon which to improve, and without a way of organizing for different customer demand scenarios, actual costs will rarely be the "should cost." Once a work place is set up for one-item-flow, I create standard work and create different versions of that standard work for different demand scenarios. **TAKT time** means "the tempo at which work has to be conducted to meet demand."

TAKT = Available Time / Demand

Classic Standard Work must consist of:

Time observations – required to determine true work content when done at a comfortable, sustainable pace. As such, it should only be determined by those who will do the work.

Equipment capacity analysis – required to determine that the available equipment is capable of producing to TAKT

Line balancing chart(s) – required to show the distribution of work among the team members, and hence, the number of staff required for a given TAKT scenario

Standard work combination sheets – one per worker per TAKT Scenario is required to show, in detail, how the work should proceed per TAKT cycle for each team member

Standard work overview sheet – required to enable basic visual management of the overall process for a given TAKT scenario

Process control board – required to enable simple, at-a-glance analysis of actual process performance vs. planned and theoretical. Also enables the team to highlight problems and their relative impact in order to sequence problem-solving and improvement efforts.

Remember, without all these pieces in place the standard work will not enable the new process to operate smoothly and the team will not have a known foundation from which to further improve. We have seen flow fail many times and most often it is due to a lack of standard work and a lack of understanding of all of required elements for standard work. Standard operating procedures (SOPs), for example, are not considered standard work in Lean circles.

5) Pull, Don't Push

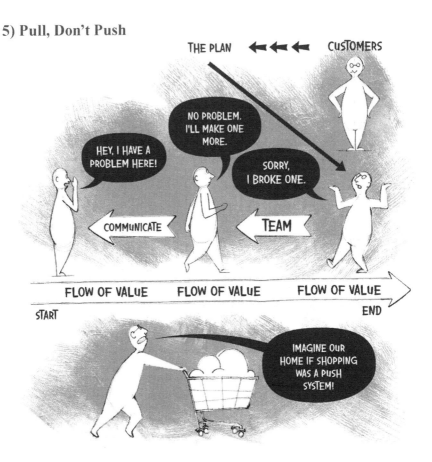

The idea is simple. The schedule for demand is sent to only one place (preferably the end of the process flow). All work is triggered or "pulled" by the downstream "customer" to their upstream "supplier" process.

The reason for this thinking is that in the real world of human work systems, problems happen. In push-based systems things don't always go according to plan, so actual output never quite matches planned demand, and vice versa. With a push system, problems cannot be adjusted for naturally like in a pull-based system. The pull system, when implemented correctly, self-compensates.

Kanban is a popular term for a pull-based work trigger. Here the implementation sequence for JIT-flow is vitally important because there must be flow before trying to pull; otherwise, the customer has to send the pull signal to a great many places at once, or the supplier has equally as many points to supply and has to build some kind of buffer (think: waste).

Sensei Question #24

How does a push-based economy inevitably result in over-consumption?

6) Visual Management and Jidoka Thinking

Once we have good flow with standard work triggered by pull systems, the "water-level" of work-in-progress that normally hides what is really happening is dramatically lowered. This immediately reveals lots more waste. Everyone close to the process will not be surprised, but to others not close to the process, it may be a shock that things do not flow well. It is at this stage of implementation that a fundamental belief must be overturned.

Many leaders and managers schooled in Craft or Mass-type process management earned their wings from being able to circumvent problems or buffer them so that they are invisible. Lean thinking, on the other hand, demands the opposite. It wants the JIT process to stop dead when problems arise. Why? To see and solve problems.

This is, of course, easier said than done when one has had a lifetime of keeping things going at all costs. In the long term we know stopping to correct revealed problems is a good thing because it means more improvement is possible, but if a person is not used to such a world it can be quite demoralizing initially. In fact, until we can solve problems as quickly as they are being revealed, life in the JIT world will be frustrating. This is where two essential elements help a great deal.

Visual management is achieved by having creative solutions within the design of the new processes that show immediately and visually if conditions are normal or abnormal. Such indicators, such as whether the process is on-target or off, shorten the time to recognize there is a problem to fix. It also means that leaders and support staff do not have to disturb the value-added workers to get straight to doing their support tasks.

For example, replenishing supplies of consumable items required by the value-added steps in the process can be done easily, silently and Just-in-Time with the right visual indicators.

Note: The standard work mentioned earlier is a must-have foundation for visual management.

Jidoka thinking is a state of mind born from the inventions of Sakichi Toyoda. His automatic weaving loom would stop immediately whenever a warp (vertical) thread snapped, and thus eliminated the chance of the machine making defective cloth. The loom achieved worldwide acclaim because it released people from the waste of babysitting machines. It also served to highlight the principle that it is better to stop and fix a problem while it is small than allow the problem to get any bigger.

With *Jidoka* devices on equipment and – more importantly – *Jidoka* thinking within people, problems can be highlighted and solved as they happen in real time, with a higher likelihood of determining the root cause. The speed of problem solving also ensures better odds at getting effective improvement. Having arrived at this stage of implementation, it is normal to see quality increase dramatically.

Sensei Question #25

The Jidoka belief means that doing nothing is better than creating waste. How can this be correct?

Sensei Question #26

As a Lean thinker, what are the best things you can do when you have nothing to do?

7) Team- and Gemba-Based Problem Solving

Once we have true one-by-one flow of value through our processes we will be revealing problems one-by-one. This is a good thing. In anything but a flow system, it makes sense for people to solve problems off-line as an individual endeavor, because there are so many problems that one has to pick and chose which ones to attempt to solve first. In a Just-In-Time Flow Process it is the opposite.

When a problem arises, the whole flow stops. With no pull signals everyone is free to join in with the problem solving which has to be done on-line in order to restart the flow. By doing this in the *Gemba* (the actual place of action) and using simple methods, the team can more likely understand the direct causes and effects of a problem and solve it.

For example, teams can ask *Why* five times to find the root cause, and then stimulate some creative solutions by asking five *Hows* for ways in which each root cause could be solved. Solutions can then be "try-stormed" and reviewed under the guidance of a coach. With a simple but nevertheless scientific method of improvement such as A3 thinking, teams can soon develop much higher numbers of people with rapid and proven problem-solving abilities. These people who are able to find and solve problems begin to create an ever-improving rate of improvement.

The rate of "improvement-of-improvement" or what I call ***Improvity*** is ultimately what should determine the long-term success of an organization.

Sensei Question #27

When do problems start to become opportunities?

Sensei Question #28

How many people will need to be good problem-solvers in the lean enterprise?

8) Cost Management with Job Security

The results of eliminating waste show up in many ways. Removing wasteful steps in a process and putting it into flow always leads to a dramatic improvement in quality and consistency. The subsequent creation of standard work for a new, less wasteful process invariably results in a need for fewer people to perform the same work than before improvement took place. So how possible is "improvement forever" if those people, now freed up, lose their jobs? In order to take our improvement to the bottom line we want every process to run at the correct staffing (and hence, the "should cost" level) for a given demand.

So how do we resolve what in most people's experience is THE human paradox of improvement?

Well, first we must immediately redeploy surplus staff to avoid improvement sliding back and gains being lost again. We must also know then exactly what capacity we now have to fill with more value-adding work. When improvement comes as rapidly as Lean drives it, the only long-term fuel for continuous improvement is growth. So as soon as progress is made, every effort should be made to sell the new capabilities and find more value-added work for people to do. A good place to look is by insourcing things that have been previously outsourced.

Previously this may have been unthinkable, but how do those previously outsourced elements of the process look when we know we are paying for both the value-added work + waste of our supplier? Also, how do they look now that we have some freed-up labor available and new lower-waste ideas about how the work could be done?

This way of thinking is often so counter to previous strategy that I teach it as mandatory: *always redeploy the top performer from the improved process.* Only this action can send the clear message that we are serious about not losing people, and if this is not immediately possible, why not have those people temporarily working on further improvement or growth?

Sensei Question #28

What would be the easiest way to fuel the growth you will need to fuel the improvement beyond the start-up phase?

9) Total Productive Maintenance

Soon after the creation of our first Just-In-Time-Flow processes, we find out very quickly just how reliable (or not) our equipment is. This is both a function of its design and maintenance.

Maintenance has evolved over the years from what I call:

a) Breakdown-based Maintenance – "It has just broken down so we have fixed it," to

b) Preventive Maintenance – "We service the equipment to planned schedules to ensure it doesn't breakdown."

In 1971, Nippondenso (A Toyota group company) was awarded a top prize for maintenance, and recognition for exceeding Preventative Maintenance by developing a new approach called **Total Productive Maintenance** (TPM). With TPM they modified their equipment to enhance its designed level of reliability to a better-than-new condition. Also, the ownership of maintenance was shared between the staff who used the equipment and the maintenance specialists. The staff did regular maintenance tasks and the specialists took on the less frequent, but required, deeper maintenance. As a team they improved their equipment to make it easier for the non-specialists to do the routine work.

Together they also realized that for a demand-triggered, JIT flow-based system, Overall Equipment Effectiveness (OEE) is a key metric. This became a new way to benchmark the effectiveness of equipment and the term OEE became the new measure: **OEE = Operational Availability x Performance Rate x Quality Rate.**

In short, only when equipment can produce the quality needed at the pace needed, and be available on demand, can that equipment be deemed fit-for-flow. TPM gets us there.

Sensei Question #30

What type of maintenance do you have at your place of work?

10) Leveling

Once the focus on the elimination of waste is established, Lean thinking also encourages us to seek to eliminate *overburdening* and *unevenness*.

This means:

1) Having a viable level of work that is achievable in the time available with the resources available,

and

2) Deliberately sequencing the work schedule opposite to the principles of economies of scale with its batch-driven thinking

Economic batch quantity-thinking **actively produces unevenness** in processes not linked to actual demand. This is termed "demand amplification" and it is a by-product of economies of scale. That is why as consumers we have partially used supplies all over our houses and why we have been conditioned to believe in deals that offer more than we need but appear to be better value. These are all pushed by economies of scales producers using mass-based processes. They have to, to make their business model work.

Conversely, once we have flow, right-sized equipment and low inventory processes, we can operate without the boom-and-bust roller coaster ride that occurs is a result of economies of scale and economic batch quantity-thinking. The end results are obvious – shorter lead times, lower inventory, higher quality, less stress for workers, less burden on suppliers. It takes a lot of un-learning to get over economies of scale beliefs, but over time we will see that variation, and its elimination, lives hand-in-hand with eliminating waste.

Batch Thinking - Requirements by different Type and make in batches

A) ΔΔΔΔΔΔ

B) ΠΠΠΠΠΠΠΠΠΠΠ

C) ◊◊◊◊

Conventional wisdom says do all B's first then the A's followed by the C's, but <u>Leveling wisdom says</u> mix equally so that routine can be made from variable demand.

◊ΠΠΔΠΠΔ◊ΠΠΔΠΠΔ◊ΠΠΔΠΠΔ◊

Sensei Question #30

What law of mass production thinking makes leveling seem so wrong?

Creating the Culture

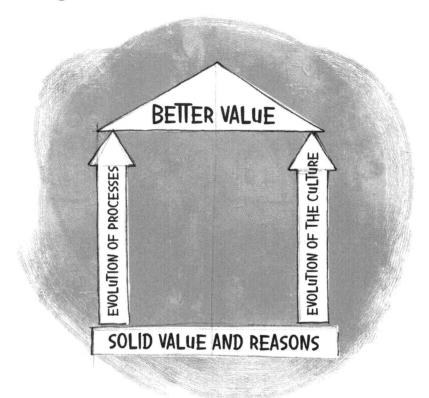

As I said earlier, the Toyota Production System was born from the Toyota Way, not the other way around, and so to create a lean enterprise **the culture** has to evolve in parallel with the way processes are changing. Essentially, Values, Habits and Beliefs will change to support the new paradigm of work if we recognize that for the transformation to be long lasting and real, this <u>must</u> happen.

Too often I have seen good transformations be negatively affected by an unsupported culture. Equally, I have heard those cast in the role of change agent getting frustrated at their leaders without adequately explaining, or attempting to teach, or even describe the alternative culture they now seek.

At the start of the book I listed six precepts required for Lean to stand a chance. Let's discuss each with regard to the specifics of *culture*. I have posed each as a sensei question in itself.

1. Are you dissatisfied with the Status Quo?

In sports, what often characterizes those at the very top of their game is an almost pathological dissatisfaction with their performances unless they can detect improvement. Always striving for and then resetting goals to a new challenge is a good habit for an organization to have. However, the sporting analogy only goes so far. "Forever improve!" is easy to say but for most mere mortals, hard to live everyday unless we truly believe it and have the skills and time to do it. In the short term a sense of crisis will always help, but remember, in the long term we need to replace the threat of impending doom with both the positive challenge of being the best and yet a collective humility, able to learn from any source.

Further, the organization needs to have opportunities to improve hard-wired into its schedule. My favorite question when I meet leadership teams is: "Of all your assumptions for planning and running this enterprise, how much time do you set aside per person each year for making hands-on, actual improvement?" I always clarify, "Not training, meetings or conferences, but actual time given to making things tangibly better?" (Guess what, in 20 years, the most given answer is?)

A highly effective way to create constant dissatisfaction with the status quo is by setting some True North goals. Unlike so-called SMART (Specific, Measurable, Achievable, Realistic, and Time-bound) objectives, True North's have a higher purpose. They are meant to energize improvement forever. Think of them not as SMART, but WISE objectives.

WAY beyond anything you can currently imagine,
Inspirational to imagine what it would be like, yet
Specific, and
Equally weighted across the four essential dimensions of enterprise performance

o   Human –zero lost people

o   Quality –zero defects

o   Time –zero waiting

o   Financial –zero waste

After setting True North goals, then allow improvement to happen by scheduling time for it in regular big change events as well as daily improvements.

2. Do you have the required Humility?

It is impossible to set and then journey toward the True North's without humility. Humility drives a deep-seated belief that there is always more to learn than we currently know, and that "if it ain't broke, we should improve it." If our culture is truly humble it will always be open to learning and improving – if that is the case, who knows what the potential might be!

3. Is Respect for People, Society and the Environment at the top of your agenda?

Respecting people for their limitless and untapped talent, the time that they give to an organization, and the potential for their engagement in an enterprises quest is required to have a culture able to wage war on waste for a lifetime. The culture has to see not only its purpose, but also its place in wider society, safe in the knowledge that it can serve that purpose without destroying the environment. All workers today exist in a sea of waste, so I propose it is actually disrespectful for each of us to not tackle it.

4. Do you believe that "Lean Will Work Wherever Work is Done"?

Leaders with a belief that "Wherever there is work, there is waste" are the key to helping others see it. If we can see waste we are halfway to removing it, but always remember, seeing is one thing, accepting we have to do something about it is another. Unfortunately, most organizations are fairly used to looking solely at operations or production departments for improvement while never considering the rest of the enterprise. I have lost count of the number of non-operations people who believe that Lean and waste, and even the need for improvement, do not apply to them. I have learned to avoid the obvious conflict and simply say, "OK, stop thinking and let's start looking for waste." Bottom line is, if we currently think Lean does not apply to our work, we need to look harder and accept the above precept.

5. Will you value GEMBA Wisdom over theoretical knowledge?

Almost every description of work, whether anecdotal or contained in a detailed procedure, can never convey what an actual day at work is like. The realities of the actual place where the work is done are only truly known by those who do it. The pioneers of Lean knew this because they were actual practitioners of improvement in the work place, not the conference room creators of a theoretical system. I have lost count of the times I have heard things described in conference rooms that turn out to be nothing like what I actually observed in the workplace.

Taiichi Ohno stressed this in a variety of ways, but my favorite quote is, "Managers should go and "read" the actual situation in the workplace." He added, "If you deal with problems on the spot when they occur, the people will feel responsible, understand and learn."

Gemba-thinking wisdom means that only in the workplace can I truly learn what the theory means. One of my early senseis always stressed, "<u>DO</u>... do not <u>think</u> in abstract, go to the *Gemba* (place of action), and <u>DO</u> improvement based on actual facts, not reports." All too often these days, PDCA, the cycle of **Plan – Do – Check – Adjust**, seems to stand for Plan – Discuss – Critique and Adjourn!

6. Do you have a leadership that believes these Precepts & Principles?

Without a doubt, the biggest single failure-mode of transformation is a lack of appropriate leadership. It is also the biggest single contributor to success. What is appropriate leadership?

Due to their early attempts to muscle the changes required in Toyota and the strikes and disruption that followed, the founders of Lean realized that they would not succeed without the engagement of the entire work force. Toyota's very damaging strikes a decade into telling people how to change led to the resignation of Toyoda San himself. Upon realizing that push- based leadership had caused the unrest, it prompted a change in approach to more of a partnership, casting leaders in the role of coach. These coaches – whose question-based reasoning subsequently stimulated thousands of personal learning cycles – have built over years of collective learning a culture of people who are genuinely seen as the most valuable asset.

For most of us this is the hardest lesson that takes the longest time to learn, whether it is a leader who has to leave behind years of conventional management-by-objectives, or workers having to get used to being responsible, not just for their work, but its improvement, too.

It takes time. Social scientists tell us real culture change will take at least a generation to achieve.

So What is the Role of the Sensei?

For most people Lean elements, principles and precepts, although easy to read and understand at an intellectual level, are in practice so counterintuitive that we all need help to employ them. For that, we need to find a sensei.

Sensei - "One who has travelled the path before"

The simplest definition of a sensei is that of a teacher but the conventional notion of a teacher is not enough. Sure, senseis will no doubt teach us stuff about Lean and its tools and techniques, but the biggest part of their role is helping us with our un-learning. For that task conventional teaching methods do not work. Instead, our sensei has to work on thoughts and beliefs and, via shared actions, ultimately change our values and habits regarding the world of work.

The sensei will coach through asking questions and guide via learning-by-doing. The students should experience just enough of the pain of change to learn, without breaking their wills or that of the enterprise. The sensei will help us reflect and be with us for a lifetime of learning as we borrow their learning curve to learn faster and with better results than a DIY-based approach. We must be very discerning in our choice of sensei.

Operating a currently "Lean system" and possessing the lessons learned from doing that is not the same as the task of removing a craft- or mass-based system and replacing it with Lean. Also, beware the many that have used lean tools and implemented a facsimile of the Toyota Production System without the cultural aspects of the Toyota Way.

Finally, I have seen many versions of *kaizen* and rapid improvement approaches, many of which are not to the model required by real world business results, and further, are not executing a magnitude of change commensurate with long-lasting culture change. So along with the culture elements, ensure your sensei can show you hard results.

Final Words

In the aftermath of worldwide financial crises, it is no coincidence that we are seeing a lot of interest in Lean. Even at my mid-life point, I have lived through enough Boom-and-Bust to realize there has to be a better way to improve. I witnessed what happened in the automation boom of the late 80's and early 90's when operations had to look technologically cool and people aspired to create workplaces that had no human beings in them. Since then, I realize I have yet to meet a machine that can do kaizen!

I also saw the I.T. boom of the 90's and 00's during which the implementation of big systems actually baked in waste, automated to the point that if the system says "no" people are powerless to give customers what they want. The last decade's credit-fueled "spend-to-improve" has created a financial disaster that will take a decades-long recovery.

Based on past experience and applying the Lean insights we now have, we know that the inevitable cutting back will also result in a lot of collateral damage to value-added steps. An example is the increasing emergence of self-service in the airline industry where we self check-in, tag our own bags and find our own way through the process, essentially doing what once was done as a service and all with no reduction in price!

If only there was another way in which improvement could be achieved without collateral damage to people or value.

Final sensei question:
Is that possible?

Enjoy the Journey!

Made in the USA
San Bernardino, CA
05 December 2013